I Got Checked and I Feel Good !

To order additional copies of this book, contact:
Xlibris
1-888-795-4274
www.Xlibris.com
Orders@Xlibris.com

Environment

Nutrition

Spiritual

Dance

Profession

Fashion

Health

Music

Politics

Beauty

Fitness

DEDICATED TO

ELEONORA VANDA RADOVAN

A LEGACY OF RESILIENCE AND ACTION!

This book is dedicated to Eleonora Vanda Radovan mother of author Linda Bonanno. A strong and determined woman that fought breast cancer fearlessly until the very end.

Jillian O'Gara

Health

Jillian's thoughts on prevention...

As a mammographer, it is part of my job to make sure women learn the importance of prevention and early breast cancer detection by getting checked. Routine mammograms are the best way of detecting breast cancer early. Also very important are clinical breast exams, performed by your primary care doctor or gynecologist alongside self breast exams. Lastly talk with your doctor and ask what your risk factors are and discuss ways of prevention according to it.

BREAST CANCER IS FOUGHT EASIER WHEN IT IS CAUGHT EARLIER AND THAT IS WHY IT IS SO IMPORTANT TO GET CHECKED!

I am a young Irish Italian woman who was born and raised in Queens. I am an outspoken person who is very friendly and very outgoing. I love trying new things I could be adventurous. I am also a mammogram tech at Zwanger-Pesiri Radiology located on Long Island and the boroughs of New York. I love spending time with loved ones and since life is very precious, we shouldn't take nothing for granted.

Jimmy Carcheta

Environmental
Health

Jimmy's thoughts on prevention...

Being the parent of a cancer survivor, I never realized the silent and invisible harm that Mother Nature could cause. It was not clear at the time the damage this was causing my son. Now, I have the ability to see that we are a product of our environment. My advice would be to get a complete in-home water filtration system in order to minimize the Consumption of contaminants. You never know when, where, or how it is going to come but making these avoidance steps is a grand stride into the right direction of prevention.

YOU ARE NOT ALONE! DO WHAT YOU NEED TO DO AND PRACTICE PREVENTION!

My profession is to acquire and grow green buildings. People spend most of their lives inside of buildings; homes, stores, offices, etc... To be exact, about 85 to 90 percent of our 24 hours are spent indoors. Therefore, indoor air quality becomes a critical issue for individuals and public health. Poor indoor air quality and pollution can cause injury to occupants, it also influences their productivity in their everyday lives. That is why green buildings are so important.

I have a passion for environmental quality and, like all parents, feel protective of my children and their future. I see my parental responsibility in a global sense and want my generation's legacy to be something much finer than global warming, deforestation, extinction of species, food and water shortages, and all the other terrifying effects of environmental neglect.

Out of this passion I founded "The Cotocon Group". An energy management consultant firm, working with large scale commercial and residential building owners & developers. With our focus on Sustainability Laws, Energy Modeling, Commissioning & Retro-Commissioning, we continue to educate our clients on how to reduce capital costs and minimize greenhouse gases (GHG). As a leader in the green building community for a decade, Cotocon brings unparalleled experience and knowledge to endure our mission which is to create sustainability for both the environment and your bottom line.

Paulina
Grgurovich

Nutrition

Paulina's thoughts on prevention...

While nourishing my body with nutrient dense healing foods I also nourished my spirit by taking control of my body through mindful eating.

I HAVE ONE THING TO SAY ABOUT MAMMOGRAMS: IT'S THE MOST LOVING THING YOU CAN DO FOR YOURSELF AND YOUR FAMILY!

With a flair for healthy and creative culinary delights, I usually pack a nutritiously powerful punch into your favorite meals! I am an Italian American New Yorker, I have a professional background in child psychology and I am a wife and mother of two wonderful children! In 2013 a life changing event shook my world, a diagnosis of stage 3 breast cancer would change my life in more ways than I ever imagined. Turning to a spiritual and positive approach to battling the disease, I had developed a daily nutritional regimen for myself, to fortify and enhance my western medical course of treatment. Two years later, "Healthy Homemade" was born; a personal wellness cooking service for people who want to ensure that healthy meals are available to them while they undergo treatment. The word has spread and now "Healthy Homemade" is a household resource for busy families all over Long Island, New York, who require their dietary needs to be enjoyed in the comfort of their home!

Chris Nardi

Fitness

Chris's thoughts on prevention...

Breast cancer prevention is necessary in this day and age. With all the uncertainty in the world, having the knowledge and preventative steps/measures is valuable to those who want to continue living a great life.

As an athlete and personal trainer, we use fitness as a means of prevention. Keeping up a fitness regimen goes a long way to ensuring that a person will live a healthy, unrestrained life. It is essential to stay fit to strengthen ourselves internally (against sickness and diseases) and externally (maintaining resilience towards physical demands and fine-tuning functional actions).

DON'T DELAY OR MAKE EXCUSES. DON'T MISS YOUR BASELINE MAMMOGRAM AND BE CONSISTENT WITH EXAMS. MAINTAINING YOUR HEALTH IS A RESPONSIBILITY AND IS ALWAYS IMPORTANT.

I am an Indonesian-American born and raised in Queens, NY. I enlisted into the US Navy after High School and went to John Jay College to study International Criminal Justice. Fitness and personal health has always been important to me, especially for the field of work I signed myself up for. I grew up with asthma, and the feeling of not being able to breathe some days made me feel useless and weak. Taking initiative, learning about my own body, and improving myself has always been a personal achievement. The day my doctor told me I no longer had asthma was one of the best days of my life.

Kim Goodlook
SeaBrook

Spiritual Health

Kim's thoughts on prevention...

My personal feedback on breast cancer prevention is to be careful of what we put in our bodies and our minds. Physical and mental health is a major factor to Cancer in general. I am a poet, mentor and motivational speaker so when I'm out there reaching out to the community I'm also informing them about how to be healthy and love yourself.

MY BEST ADVICE FOR A WOMAN IN DISTRESS ABOUT HAVING A MAMMOGRAM IS THAT THE BEST THING THAT COULD HAPPEN OUT OF A BAD RESULT, IS THAT IT WAS DETECTED IN TIME TO HEAL FROM IT.

I am in an artist, an activist, a survivor, a mentor, a poet, writer and a true inspiration. The words that I speaks are of truth, hope and empowerment. Many people of all ages, races and genders truly admire the positivity and great energy that I can bring out naturally while speaking or performing. I am very well known for reaching out to my community and making a difference in this crazy world we live in by being that voice that so many are afraid to be. Giving you hope, power and a perspective from all walks of life.

Chante Jordan

Profession

Chante's thoughts on prevention…

Breast cancer detection and prevention has evolved along with the technology used to screen women. It's still a tough battle but the many warriors and champions of breast cancer have increasingly pushed the needle to broaden the age for screening, pushing for bills like Shannon's law meant to lower mammogram age to 35 and canvassing communities to educate everyone encouraging action. I truly believe we are on the cusp of a major breakthrough in science, treatment and detection for breast cancer patients.

Being the director of Public relations at a large radiology company, breast cancer affects how I interact with a patient waiting for screening or diagnostic mammogram results. In my line of work, I see women everyday filled with anxiety as they wait to be screened. Reassurance that the patient is taking control of their health just by being screened is step 1. It affects how kind, empathetic and considerate you are of someone's loved one, spouse or child offering comfort during a time of uncertainty.

PEOPLE SHOULD BE AFRAID OF CANCER NOT MAMMOGRAMS. I STRONGLY ENCOURAGE WOMEN TO GET THEIR YEARLY EXAMS.

I'm a 29yr old African American female, born and raised on Long Island and a recent transplant to Brooklyn. With a background in PR and mass communication, I'm passionate about Public Relations at Zwanger-Pesiri and look forward to working closely with an impactful movement like the "got checked?" campaign.

Joe Sappah

Music

Joe's thoughts on prevention…

I think breast cancer prevention is a key component to ones overall health and it's empowering to have some level of education and awareness. I experienced this first hand at work when a colleague of mine was diagnosed with breast cancer about two years ago. She's a survivor and happens to be one of the brightest souls I've ever met.

I WOULD ADVISE WOMEN TO CONSULT WITH THEIR PHYSICIAN AND INQUIRE ABOUT A MAMMOGRAM FINDING OUT EARLY THEIR RISK FACTORS.

I'm the single father of a 16 year old girl. A horticulturist by trade, writer, performer, poet and a recording artist as well. I'm currently signed to Chuck D's record label.

Thomasina
Ogden

Dance

Thomasina's thoughts
on prevention…

Breast cancer is so prevalent where I live these days yet I believe so much could be prevented. Early detection is the key! As a dance teacher, body image and health have been of great importance to me personally as well as a mantra to inspire students at my dance studio.

MY ADVISE TO FIRST-TIME MAMMOGRAM LADIES…EVEN THOUGH NOBODY EVER TELLS YOU "IT WAS FUN OR IT DIDN'T HURT AT ALL" —BUCK UP AND GO ANYWAY! BE IN CHARGE OF YOUR OWN DESTINY!

I was born and raised in Broad Channel, NY. I chose to open my business in my hometown so I could share my love of dance with my friends and neighbors. I have been married for 40 years to my high school sweetheart, I'm a mother of two and a grandmother to two granddaughters. In my spare time, I love to paint, craft and go antique hunting.

Pavi Manzanero

Beauty

Pavi's thoughts on prevention…

I am a firm believer that prevention is better than to cure therefore what we put in our bodies are simply our responsibilities. One obvious way of preventing breast cancer is eating healthier by including more fruits and vegetables in your diet. Personally speaking, I try to stay away from unhealthy and processed foods; I have noticed that my skin started to glow also because of the natural products I have been using. As women, this plays a vital role since cosmetics are part of our daily routine. So, imagine your skin can look like they eat fruits and vegetables, too!

GET SCREENED REGULARLY, YOU WILL BECOME A ROLE MODEL, YOUR FRIENDS AND FAMILY WILL BE ENCOURAGED TO DO THE SAME. THEREFORE, YOU ARE HELPING TO SAVE LIVES TOO!

As a paralegal primarily and also working in the beauty industry, I must have a solid knowledge of legal terminology, federal and state rules and regulations, in order to be effective. Same with prevention, without having a solid knowledge of "getting checked" by specialist or by my gynecologist regularly, I would be blinded as to what is happening inside me, therefore turning a blind eye from the truth that could possibly harm me in the end.

Linda Bonanno
And Donna Cioffi

Fashion

Linda and Donna's thoughts on prevention...

Action not awareness is our motto! We are the founders of the "got checked?" campaign and the pioneers of breast health education in a nutshell. We are adamant at using every tool to encourage the next generation to practice prevention. We are developing the building blocks of breast health in NYS and soon nationally, creating an easy plan of action for today's busy woman. A lifestyle campaign with a subliminal message, whether it is with literature, music, or fashion we communicate effectively the importance of a balanced mind, body, and soul. Feeling good allows your "best you" to inspire the world.

TAKE CHARGE OF YOUR LIFE TODAY AND PRACTICE ACTION... WRITE YOUR DESTINY ACCORDING TO YOUR NEEDS AND WANTS.. IT STARTS WITH YOU, MAKE A MOVE!

Donna Cioffi- I am the president of "First Company Pink" a non-profit and co- founder of the "got checked?" campaign, whose missions is focused on breast health education and early prevention. I am a mother of 3 and a survivor who is extremely dedicated to reinforce the importance of early intervention with a campaign that aims to remain current and progressive; while constantly seeking social, political and educational changes.

Linda Bonanno- I am the Vice President of "First Company Pink" a non-profit and co-founder of the "got checked?" campaign. I am a mother of 2 and a survivor. I am very much committed to youth and educating, using innovating tools and approachable methods. Literature, music, videos and everything related to the new technology and social media era are used to penetrate young minds in a subliminal way.

Shanequa
Charles

Politics

Shanequa's thoughts on prevention...

One of the leading facts about breast cancer screening that stands out to me the most is that prevention assures a stronger possibility of LIFE. Almost 7 years ago my beloved mother left this earth because of 4th stage lung cancer, metastatic matter in all four regions of her brain left her unable to fight, a loss of a woman still full of life.

PREVENTION AND REGULAR SCREENINGS PUT THE POWER OF LIFE BACK INTO YOUR HANDS. ALLOWING YOU AND YOUR FAMILIES TO ENJOY THE PRECIOUS TIME ON THIS EARTH THAT WE ARE SUPPOSED TO ENJOY. IT KEEPS GRANDMAS AROUND FOR THEIR GRANDBABIES, MOMS ABLE TO WATCH THEIR CHILDREN GROW, THE VILLAGE IN TACT... BECAUSE A WOMANLESS VILLAGE IS NOT A VILLAGE !

I am the Executive Director of Miss Abbie's Kids, a youth development nonprofit servicing the North East Bronx and abroad whose goal is to build a stronger more sustainable Bronx child through real world teachings. I also am the co-founder of Never Be Caged, a newly formed coalition that seeks to end mass incarceration through investment in our youth. I am an mother, activist and rebel organizer, who works alongside many others on city, state and federal level legislation in order to sustain freedoms for people of color, marginalized communities and communities experiencing poverty. My daughter, Miracle Robinson has been a mother leading force in the fight for freedom and justice as an entrepreneur who uses her proceeds to address and eliminate hunger amongst homeless children in NYC. To follow our work, please go to NeverBeCaged.org and StyledByMiracle.com.

Ask about your family history on both mother and father side...
Is genetic testing an option for you?

_____

_____

_____

_____

_____

_____

_____

_____

_____

_____

_____

Now take action and share with your doctor...

Self examination…
How to preform a self breast exam
How to preform a self chest exam

Breast/Chest Self Examination *ITS EASY! GET IT DONE!*

Women and men of all ages are encouraged to perform breast self-exams at least once a month. Breast self-exams help you to be familiar with how your breasts look and feel so you can alert your healthcare professional if there are any changes.

The best time to do a monthly self-breast exam is about 3 to 5 days after your period starts. Do it at the same time every month. Your breasts are not as tender or lumpy at this time in your monthly cycle.

HOW TO GET STARTED:

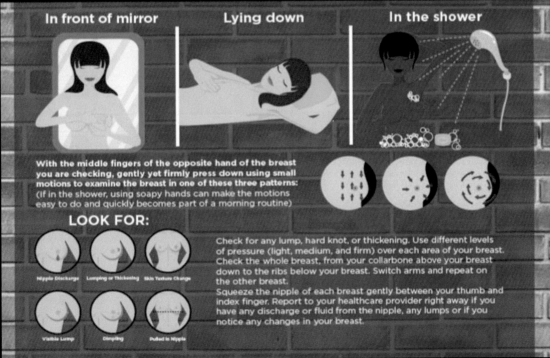

In front of mirror   **Lying down**   **In the shower**

With the middle fingers of the opposite hand of the breast you are checking, gently yet firmly press down using small motions to examine the breast in one of these three patterns: (If in the shower, using soapy hands can make the motions easy to do and quickly becomes part of a morning routine)

LOOK FOR:

Nipple Discharge   Lumping or Thickening   Skin Texture Change

Visible Lump   Dimpling   Pulled in Nipple

Check for any lump, hard knot, or thickening. Use different levels of pressure (light, medium, and firm) over each area of your breast. Check the whole breast, from your collarbone above your breast down to the ribs below your breast. Switch arms and repeat on the other breast.
Squeeze the nipple of each breast gently between your thumb and index finger. Report to your healthcare provider right away if you have any discharge or fluid from the nipple, any lumps or if you notice any changes in your breast.

Now take action and get it done!

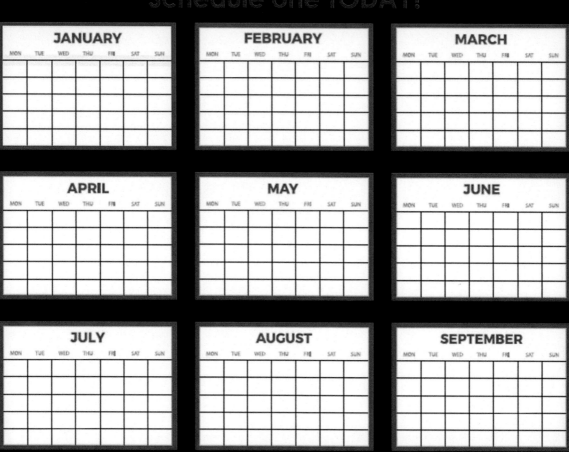

JANUARY	FEBRUARY	MARCH
MON TUE WED THU FRI SAT SUN	MON TUE WED THU FRI SAT SUN	MON TUE WED THU FRI SAT SUN

APRIL	MAY	JUNE
MON TUE WED THU FRI SAT SUN	MON TUE WED THU FRI SAT SUN	MON TUE WED THU FRI SAT SUN

JULY	AUGUST	SEPTEMBER
MON TUE WED THU FRI SAT SUN	MON TUE WED THU FRI SAT SUN	MON TUE WED THU FRI SAT SUN

OCTOBER	NOVEMBER	DECEMBER
MON TUE WED THU FRI SAT SUN	MON TUE WED THU FRI SAT SUN	MON TUE WED THU FRI SAT SUN

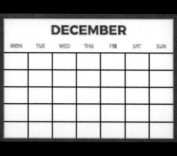

Note to self:

_____

_____

_____

_____

_____

_____

_____

_____

_____

_____

_____

_____

Note to self:

_____

_____

_____

_____

_____

_____

_____

_____

_____

_____

_____

Note to self:

_____

_____

_____

_____

_____

_____

_____

_____

_____

_____

_____

_____

Acknowledgements

Editorial:

Shavana Jonathan

Contributors:

Jillian O'Gara

Jimmy Carcheta

Paulina Grgurovich

Chris Nardi

Kim Goodlook Seabrook

Chante Jordan

Joe Sappah

Thomasina Ogden

Pavi Manzanero

Linda Bonanno

Donna Cioffi

Shanequa Charles

Photographer

Gary Freemon at Free Money Films

Cover Art and Illustrations

Doris Jelinek

Printed in the United States
By Bookmasters